Journal

Owner

Name: ______________________________

How to Get Out of Your Comfort Zone

1. Set a Goal

Taking action is the most important part of getting out of your comfort zone. Once you start taking steps towards your goal, you'll find it becomes easier and more enjoyable.

2. Make a plan

Making a plan is key to achieving your goal. Breaking down your goal into smaller steps will make it feel more manageable and less daunting.

3. Take Action

Taking action is the most important part of getting out of your comfort zone. Once you start taking steps towards your goal, you'll find it becomes easier and more enjoyable.

4. Be Persistent

Don't give up if you don't achieve your goal right away. Be persistent and keep working towards it.

The best
investment
that you can
make is in
yourself.

2024
January

Sun	Mon	Tue	Wed	Thu	Fri	Sat
	1	2	3	4	5	6
7	8	9	10	11	12	13
14	15	16	17	18	19	20
21	22	23	24	25	26	27
28	29	30	31			

Monthly
BUDGET PLAN

MONTH:

____

INCOME

DATE	DESCRIPTION	AMOUNT

FIXED EXPENSES

DATE	DESCRIPTION	AMOUNT

OTHER EXPENSES

DATE	DESCRIPTION	AMOUNT

TOTAL:

Weekly
BUDGET PLAN

WEEK:

____

MONDAY AMOUNT: | EXPENSES:

TUESDAY AMOUNT: | EXPENSES:

WEDNESDAY AMOUNT: | EXPENSES:

THRUSDAY AMOUNT: | EXPENSES:

FRIDAY AMOUNT: | EXPENSES:

SATURDAY AMOUNT: | EXPENSES:

SUNDAY AMOUNT:1 | EXPENSES:

TOTAL:

Weekly
BUDGET PLAN

WEEK: _______________

MONDAY AMOUNT: | EXPENSES:

TUESDAY AMOUNT: | EXPENSES:

WEDNESDAY AMOUNT: | EXPENSES:

THRUSDAY AMOUNT: | EXPENSES:

FRIDAY AMOUNT: | EXPENSES:

SATURDAY AMOUNT: | EXPENSES:

SUNDAY AMOUNT:1 | EXPENSES:

TOTAL:

Weekly
BUDGET PLAN

WEEK: _______________

MONDAY AMOUNT: | EXPENSES:

TUESDAY AMOUNT: | EXPENSES:

WEDNESDAY AMOUNT: | EXPENSES:

THRUSDAY AMOUNT: | EXPENSES:

FRIDAY AMOUNT: | EXPENSES:

SATURDAY AMOUNT: | EXPENSES:

SUNDAY AMOUNT:1 | EXPENSES:

TOTAL:

Weekly
BUDGET PLAN

WEEK:

____

MONDAY AMOUNT: | EXPENSES:

TUESDAY AMOUNT: | EXPENSES:

WEDNESDAY AMOUNT: | EXPENSES:

THRUSDAY AMOUNT: | EXPENSES:

FRIDAY AMOUNT: | EXPENSES:

SATURDAY AMOUNT: | EXPENSES:

SUNDAY AMOUNT:1 | EXPENSES:

TOTAL:

FOR SPECIAL

notes

FOR SPECIAL

FOR SPECIAL

notes

2024
February

Sun	Mon	Tue	Wed	Thu	Fri	Sat
				1	2	3
4	5	6	7	8	9	10
11	12	13	14	15	16	17
18	19	20	21	22	23	24
25	26	27	28	29		

NOTES :

Monthly
BUDGET PLAN

MONTH:

____

INCOME

DATE	DESCRIPTION	AMOUNT

FIXED EXPENSES

DATE	DESCRIPTION	AMOUNT

OTHER EXPENSES

DATE	DESCRIPTION	AMOUNT

TOTAL:

Weekly
BUDGET PLAN

WEEK:

____

MONDAY AMOUNT: EXPENSES:

TUESDAY
AMOUNT: EXPENSES:

WEDNESDAY
AMOUNT: EXPENSES:

THRUSDAY
AMOUNT: EXPENSES:

FRIDAY AMOUNT: EXPENSES:

SATURDAY
AMOUNT: EXPENSES:

SUNDAY
AMOUNT:1   EXPENSES:

TOTAL:

Weekly
BUDGET PLAN

WEEK:
____

MONDAY AMOUNT: | EXPENSES:

TUESDAY AMOUNT: | EXPENSES:

WEDNESDAY AMOUNT: | EXPENSES:

THRUSDAY AMOUNT: | EXPENSES:

FRIDAY AMOUNT: | EXPENSES:

SATURDAY AMOUNT: | EXPENSES:

SUNDAY AMOUNT:1 | EXPENSES:

TOTAL:

Weekly
BUDGET PLAN

WEEK:

____

MONDAY AMOUNT: | EXPENSES:

TUESDAY AMOUNT: | EXPENSES:

WEDNESDAY AMOUNT: | EXPENSES:

THRUSDAY AMOUNT: | EXPENSES:

FRIDAY AMOUNT: | EXPENSES:

SATURDAY AMOUNT: | EXPENSES:

SUNDAY AMOUNT:I | EXPENSES:

TOTAL:

Weekly
BUDGET PLAN

WEEK:

MONDAY AMOUNT: | EXPENSES:

TUESDAY AMOUNT: | EXPENSES:

WEDNESDAY AMOUNT: | EXPENSES:

THRUSDAY AMOUNT: | EXPENSES:

FRIDAY AMOUNT: | EXPENSES:

SATURDAY AMOUNT: | EXPENSES:

SUNDAY AMOUNT:1 | EXPENSES:

TOTAL:

2024
March

Sun	Mon	Tue	Wed	Thu	Fri	Sat
					1	2
3	4	5	6	7	8	9
10	11	12	13	14	15	16
17	18	19	20	21	22	23
24	25	26	27	28	29	30
31						

NOTES :

Monthly
BUDGET PLAN

MONTH: _______________________

INCOME

DATE	DESCRIPTION	AMOUNT

FIXED EXPENSES

DATE	DESCRIPTION	AMOUNT

OTHER EXPENSES

DATE	DESCRIPTION	AMOUNT

TOTAL:

Weekly
BUDGET PLAN

WEEK: _______________________

MONDAY AMOUNT: | EXPENSES:

TUESDAY AMOUNT: | EXPENSES:

WEDNESDAY AMOUNT: | EXPENSES:

THRUSDAY AMOUNT: | EXPENSES:

FRIDAY AMOUNT: | EXPENSES:

SATURDAY AMOUNT: | EXPENSES:

SUNDAY AMOUNT:I | EXPENSES:

TOTAL:

Weekly
BUDGET PLAN

WEEK: _______________

MONDAY AMOUNT: | EXPENSES:

TUESDAY AMOUNT: | EXPENSES:

WEDNESDAY AMOUNT: | EXPENSES:

THRUSDAY AMOUNT: | EXPENSES:

FRIDAY AMOUNT: | EXPENSES:

SATURDAY AMOUNT: | EXPENSES:

SUNDAY AMOUNT:1 | EXPENSES:

TOTAL:

Weekly
BUDGET PLAN

WEEK: ___________________

MONDAY AMOUNT: | EXPENSES:

TUESDAY AMOUNT: | EXPENSES:

WEDNESDAY AMOUNT: | EXPENSES:

THRUSDAY AMOUNT: | EXPENSES:

FRIDAY AMOUNT: | EXPENSES:

SATURDAY AMOUNT: | EXPENSES:

SUNDAY AMOUNT:1 | EXPENSES:

TOTAL:

Weekly
BUDGET PLAN

WEEK: _______________

MONDAY AMOUNT: | EXPENSES:

TUESDAY AMOUNT: | EXPENSES:

WEDNESDAY AMOUNT: | EXPENSES:

THRUSDAY AMOUNT: | EXPENSES:

FRIDAY AMOUNT: | EXPENSES:

SATURDAY AMOUNT: | EXPENSES:

SUNDAY AMOUNT:1 | EXPENSES:

TOTAL:

FOR SPECIAL

notes

2024
April

Sun	Mon	Tue	Wed	Thu	Fri	Sat
	1	2	3	4	5	6
7	8	9	10	11	12	13
14	15	16	17	18	19	20
21	22	23	24	25	26	27
28	29	30				

Monthly
BUDGET PLAN

MONTH: ______________________

INCOME

DATE	DESCRIPTION	AMOUNT

FIXED EXPENSES

DATE	DESCRIPTION	AMOUNT

OTHER EXPENSES

DATE	DESCRIPTION	AMOUNT

TOTAL:

Weekly
BUDGET PLAN

WEEK: ______________________

MONDAY AMOUNT: | EXPENSES:

TUESDAY AMOUNT: | EXPENSES:

WEDNESDAY AMOUNT: | EXPENSES:

THRUSDAY AMOUNT: | EXPENSES:

FRIDAY AMOUNT: | EXPENSES:

SATURDAY AMOUNT: | EXPENSES:

SUNDAY AMOUNT:l | EXPENSES:

TOTAL:

Weekly
BUDGET PLAN

WEEK: ____________________

MONDAY AMOUNT: | EXPENSES:

TUESDAY AMOUNT: | EXPENSES:

WEDNESDAY AMOUNT: | EXPENSES:

THRUSDAY AMOUNT: | EXPENSES:

FRIDAY AMOUNT: | EXPENSES:

SATURDAY AMOUNT: | EXPENSES:

SUNDAY AMOUNT:1 | EXPENSES:

TOTAL:

Weekly
BUDGET PLAN

WEEK:

____

MONDAY AMOUNT: | EXPENSES:

TUESDAY AMOUNT: | EXPENSES:

WEDNESDAY AMOUNT: | EXPENSES:

THRUSDAY AMOUNT: | EXPENSES:

FRIDAY AMOUNT: | EXPENSES:

SATURDAY AMOUNT: | EXPENSES:

SUNDAY AMOUNT:1 | EXPENSES:

TOTAL:

Weekly

BUDGET PLAN

WEEK:

____

MONDAY AMOUNT: | EXPENSES:

TUESDAY AMOUNT: | EXPENSES:

WEDNESDAY AMOUNT: | EXPENSES:

THRUSDAY AMOUNT: | EXPENSES:

FRIDAY AMOUNT: | EXPENSES:

SATURDAY AMOUNT: | EXPENSES:

SUNDAY AMOUNT:1 | EXPENSES:

TOTAL:

FOR SPECIAL

notes

2024 May

Sun	Mon	Tue	Wed	Thu	Fri	Sat
			1	2	3	4
5	6	7	8	9	10	11
12	13	14	15	16	17	18
19	20	21	22	23	24	25
26	27	28	29	30	31	

Monthly
BUDGET PLAN

MONTH: _______________________

INCOME

DATE	DESCRIPTION	AMOUNT

FIXED EXPENSES

DATE	DESCRIPTION	AMOUNT

OTHER EXPENSES

DATE	DESCRIPTION	AMOUNT

TOTAL:

Weekly
BUDGET PLAN

WEEK:
____

MONDAY AMOUNT: | EXPENSES:

TUESDAY AMOUNT: | EXPENSES:

WEDNESDAY AMOUNT: | EXPENSES:

THRUSDAY AMOUNT: | EXPENSES:

FRIDAY AMOUNT: | EXPENSES:

SATURDAY AMOUNT: | EXPENSES:

SUNDAY AMOUNT:1 | EXPENSES:

TOTAL:

Weekly
BUDGET PLAN

WEEK: _______________

MONDAY AMOUNT: EXPENSES:

TUESDAY
AMOUNT: EXPENSES:

WEDNESDAY
AMOUNT: EXPENSES:

THRUSDAY
AMOUNT: EXPENSES:

FRIDAY AMOUNT: EXPENSES:

SATURDAY
AMOUNT: EXPENSES:

SUNDAY
AMOUNT:1   EXPENSES:

TOTAL:

Weekly
BUDGET PLAN

WEEK: _______________________

MONDAY AMOUNT: | EXPENSES:

TUESDAY AMOUNT: | EXPENSES:

WEDNESDAY AMOUNT: | EXPENSES:

THRUSDAY AMOUNT: | EXPENSES:

FRIDAY AMOUNT: | EXPENSES:

SATURDAY AMOUNT: | EXPENSES:

SUNDAY AMOUNT:1 | EXPENSES:

TOTAL:

Weekly
BUDGET PLAN

WEEK: ________________

MONDAY AMOUNT: EXPENSES:

TUESDAY
AMOUNT: EXPENSES:

WEDNESDAY
AMOUNT: EXPENSES:

THRUSDAY
AMOUNT: EXPENSES:

FRIDAY AMOUNT: EXPENSES:

SATURDAY
AMOUNT: EXPENSES:

SUNDAY
AMOUNT:1   EXPENSES:

TOTAL:

FOR SPECIAL

notes

FOR SPECIAL

notes

2024 June

Sun	Mon	Tue	Wed	Thu	Fri	Sat
						1
2	3	4	5	6	7	8
9	10	11	12	13	14	15
16	17	18	19	20	21	22
23	24	25	26	27	28	29
30						

Monthly
BUDGET PLAN

MONTH:

INCOME

DATE	DESCRIPTION	AMOUNT

FIXED EXPENSES

DATE	DESCRIPTION	AMOUNT

OTHER EXPENSES

DATE	DESCRIPTION	AMOUNT

TOTAL:

Weekly
BUDGET PLAN

WEEK:

____

MONDAY AMOUNT: | EXPENSES:

TUESDAY AMOUNT: | EXPENSES:

WEDNESDAY AMOUNT: | EXPENSES:

THRUSDAY AMOUNT: | EXPENSES:

FRIDAY AMOUNT: | EXPENSES:

SATURDAY AMOUNT: | EXPENSES:

SUNDAY AMOUNT: | EXPENSES:

TOTAL:

Weekly
BUDGET PLAN

WEEK: ______________________

MONDAY AMOUNT: | EXPENSES:

TUESDAY AMOUNT: | EXPENSES:

WEDNESDAY AMOUNT: | EXPENSES:

THRUSDAY AMOUNT: | EXPENSES:

FRIDAY AMOUNT: | EXPENSES:

SATURDAY AMOUNT: | EXPENSES:

SUNDAY AMOUNT:1 | EXPENSES:

TOTAL:

Weekly
BUDGET PLAN

WEEK:

____

MONDAY AMOUNT: | EXPENSES:

TUESDAY AMOUNT: | EXPENSES:

WEDNESDAY AMOUNT: | EXPENSES:

THRUSDAY AMOUNT: | EXPENSES:

FRIDAY AMOUNT: | EXPENSES:

SATURDAY AMOUNT: | EXPENSES:

SUNDAY AMOUNT:1 | EXPENSES:

TOTAL:

Weekly
BUDGET PLAN

WEEK: _______________

MONDAY AMOUNT: | EXPENSES:

TUESDAY AMOUNT: | EXPENSES:

WEDNESDAY AMOUNT: | EXPENSES:

THRUSDAY AMOUNT: | EXPENSES:

FRIDAY AMOUNT: | EXPENSES:

SATURDAY AMOUNT: | EXPENSES:

SUNDAY AMOUNT:1 | EXPENSES:

TOTAL:

notes

FOR SPECIAL

notes

2024
July

Sun	Mon	Tue	Wed	Thu	Fri	Sat
	1	2	3	4	5	6
7	8	9	10	11	12	13
14	15	16	17	18	19	20
21	22	23	24	25	26	27
28	29	30	31			

Monthly
BUDGET PLAN

MONTH: ________________________

INCOME

DATE	DESCRIPTION	AMOUNT

FIXED EXPENSES

DATE	DESCRIPTION	AMOUNT

OTHER EXPENSES

DATE	DESCRIPTION	AMOUNT

TOTAL:

Weekly
BUDGET PLAN

WEEK: _______________________

MONDAY AMOUNT: EXPENSES:

TUESDAY
AMOUNT: EXPENSES:

WEDNESDAY
AMOUNT: EXPENSES:

THRUSDAY
AMOUNT: EXPENSES:

FRIDAY AMOUNT: EXPENSES:

SATURDAY
AMOUNT: EXPENSES:

SUNDAY
AMOUNT:1   EXPENSES:

TOTAL:

Weekly
BUDGET PLAN

WEEK:

____

MONDAY AMOUNT: EXPENSES:

TUESDAY
AMOUNT: EXPENSES:

WEDNESDAY
AMOUNT: EXPENSES:

THRUSDAY
AMOUNT: EXPENSES:

FRIDAY AMOUNT: EXPENSES:

SATURDAY
AMOUNT: EXPENSES:

SUNDAY
AMOUNT:1   EXPENSES:

TOTAL:

Weekly
BUDGET PLAN

WEEK:

____

MONDAY AMOUNT:

EXPENSES:

TUESDAY AMOUNT:

EXPENSES:

WEDNESDAY AMOUNT:

EXPENSES:

THRUSDAY AMOUNT:

EXPENSES:

FRIDAY AMOUNT:

EXPENSES:

SATURDAY AMOUNT:

EXPENSES:

SUNDAY AMOUNT:1

EXPENSES:

TOTAL:

Weekly
BUDGET PLAN

WEEK: ______________________

MONDAY AMOUNT:

EXPENSES:

TUESDAY
AMOUNT:

EXPENSES:

WEDNESDAY
AMOUNT:

EXPENSES:

THRUSDAY
AMOUNT:

EXPENSES:

FRIDAY AMOUNT:

EXPENSES:

SATURDAY
AMOUNT:

EXPENSES:

SUNDAY
AMOUNT:1

EXPENSES:

TOTAL:

FOR SPECIAL

2024
August

Sun	Mon	Tue	Wed	Thu	Fri	Sat
				1	2	3
4	5	6	7	8	9	10
11	12	13	14	15	16	17
18	19	20	21	22	23	24
25	26	27	28	29	30	31

Monthly
BUDGET PLAN

MONTH:

INCOME

DATE	DESCRIPTION	AMOUNT

FIXED EXPENSES

DATE	DESCRIPTION	AMOUNT

OTHER EXPENSES

DATE	DESCRIPTION	AMOUNT

TOTAL:

Weekly
BUDGET PLAN

WEEK: ______________________

MONDAY AMOUNT: | EXPENSES:

TUESDAY AMOUNT: | EXPENSES:

WEDNESDAY AMOUNT: | EXPENSES:

THRUSDAY AMOUNT: | EXPENSES:

FRIDAY AMOUNT: | EXPENSES:

SATURDAY AMOUNT: | EXPENSES:

SUNDAY AMOUNT:1 | EXPENSES:

TOTAL:

Weekly
BUDGET PLAN

WEEK:

____

MONDAY AMOUNT: | EXPENSES:

TUESDAY AMOUNT: | EXPENSES:

WEDNESDAY AMOUNT: | EXPENSES:

THRUSDAY AMOUNT: | EXPENSES:

FRIDAY AMOUNT: | EXPENSES:

SATURDAY AMOUNT: | EXPENSES:

SUNDAY AMOUNT:1 | EXPENSES:

TOTAL:

Weekly
BUDGET PLAN

WEEK: _______________________

MONDAY AMOUNT: | EXPENSES:

TUESDAY AMOUNT: | EXPENSES:

WEDNESDAY AMOUNT: | EXPENSES:

THRUSDAY AMOUNT: | EXPENSES:

FRIDAY AMOUNT: | EXPENSES:

SATURDAY AMOUNT: | EXPENSES:

SUNDAY AMOUNT:1 | EXPENSES:

TOTAL:

Weekly
BUDGET PLAN

WEEK: _______________

MONDAY AMOUNT: | EXPENSES:

TUESDAY AMOUNT: | EXPENSES:

WEDNESDAY AMOUNT: | EXPENSES:

THRUSDAY AMOUNT: | EXPENSES:

FRIDAY AMOUNT: | EXPENSES:

SATURDAY AMOUNT: | EXPENSES:

SUNDAY AMOUNT:1 | EXPENSES:

TOTAL:

FOR SPECIAL
notes

FOR SPECIAL

2024 September

Sun	Mon	Tue	Wed	Thu	Fri	Sat
1	2	3	4	5	6	7
8	9	10	11	12	13	14
15	16	17	18	19	20	21
22	23	24	25	26	27	28
29	30					

Monthly
BUDGET PLAN

MONTH:

____

INCOME

DATE	DESCRIPTION	AMOUNT

FIXED EXPENSES

DATE	DESCRIPTION	AMOUNT

OTHER EXPENSES

DATE	DESCRIPTION	AMOUNT

TOTAL:

Weekly
BUDGET PLAN

WEEK: _______________________

MONDAY AMOUNT: | EXPENSES:

TUESDAY
AMOUNT: | EXPENSES:

WEDNESDAY
AMOUNT: | EXPENSES:

THRUSDAY
AMOUNT: | EXPENSES:

FRIDAY AMOUNT: | EXPENSES:

SATURDAY
AMOUNT: | EXPENSES:

SUNDAY
AMOUNT:1 | EXPENSES:

TOTAL:

Weekly
BUDGET PLAN

WEEK: _______________________

MONDAY AMOUNT: | EXPENSES:

TUESDAY AMOUNT: | EXPENSES:

WEDNESDAY AMOUNT: | EXPENSES:

THRUSDAY AMOUNT: | EXPENSES:

FRIDAY AMOUNT: | EXPENSES:

SATURDAY AMOUNT: | EXPENSES:

SUNDAY AMOUNT:1 | EXPENSES:

TOTAL:

Weekly
BUDGET PLAN

WEEK: ______________________

MONDAY AMOUNT: | EXPENSES:

TUESDAY
AMOUNT: | EXPENSES:

WEDNESDAY
AMOUNT: | EXPENSES:

THRUSDAY
AMOUNT: | EXPENSES:

FRIDAY AMOUNT: | EXPENSES:

SATURDAY
AMOUNT: | EXPENSES:

SUNDAY
AMOUNT:1 | EXPENSES:

TOTAL:

Weekly
BUDGET PLAN

WEEK:

____

MONDAY AMOUNT: EXPENSES:

TUESDAY
AMOUNT: EXPENSES:

WEDNESDAY
AMOUNT: EXPENSES:

THRUSDAY
AMOUNT: EXPENSES:

FRIDAY AMOUNT: EXPENSES:

SATURDAY
AMOUNT: EXPENSES:

SUNDAY
AMOUNT:1   EXPENSES:

TOTAL:

2024
October

Sun	Mon	Tue	Wed	Thu	Fri	Sat
		1	2	3	4	5
6	7	8	9	10	11	12
13	14	15	16	17	18	19
20	21	22	23	24	25	26
27	28	29	30	31		

Monthly
BUDGET PLAN

MONTH: ___________________

INCOME

DATE	DESCRIPTION	AMOUNT

FIXED EXPENSES

DATE	DESCRIPTION	AMOUNT

OTHER EXPENSES

DATE	DESCRIPTION	AMOUNT

TOTAL:

Weekly
BUDGET PLAN

WEEK: ___________________

MONDAY AMOUNT: | EXPENSES:

TUESDAY AMOUNT: | EXPENSES:

WEDNESDAY AMOUNT: | EXPENSES:

THRUSDAY AMOUNT: | EXPENSES:

FRIDAY AMOUNT: | EXPENSES:

SATURDAY AMOUNT: | EXPENSES:

SUNDAY AMOUNT:1 | EXPENSES:

TOTAL:

Weekly
BUDGET PLAN

WEEK:

____

MONDAY AMOUNT: | EXPENSES:

TUESDAY AMOUNT: | EXPENSES:

WEDNESDAY AMOUNT: | EXPENSES:

THRUSDAY AMOUNT: | EXPENSES:

FRIDAY AMOUNT: | EXPENSES:

SATURDAY AMOUNT: | EXPENSES:

SUNDAY AMOUNT:1 | EXPENSES:

TOTAL:

Weekly
BUDGET PLAN

WEEK: _______________

MONDAY AMOUNT: | EXPENSES:

TUESDAY
AMOUNT: | EXPENSES:

WEDNESDAY
AMOUNT: | EXPENSES:

THRUSDAY
AMOUNT: | EXPENSES:

FRIDAY AMOUNT: | EXPENSES:

SATURDAY
AMOUNT: | EXPENSES:

SUNDAY
AMOUNT:1 | EXPENSES:

TOTAL:

Weekly
BUDGET PLAN

WEEK:

MONDAY AMOUNT: EXPENSES:

TUESDAY
AMOUNT: EXPENSES:

WEDNESDAY
AMOUNT: EXPENSES:

THRUSDAY
AMOUNT: EXPENSES:

FRIDAY AMOUNT: EXPENSES:

SATURDAY
AMOUNT: EXPENSES:

SUNDAY
AMOUNT:1   EXPENSES:

TOTAL:

FOR SPECIAL

notes

2024
November

Sun	Mon	Tue	Wed	Thu	Fri	Sat
					1	2
3	4	5	6	7	8	9
10	11	12	13	14	15	16
17	18	19	20	21	22	23
24	25	26	27	28	29	30

Monthly
BUDGET PLAN

MONTH: ______________________

INCOME

DATE	DESCRIPTION	AMOUNT

FIXED EXPENSES

DATE	DESCRIPTION	AMOUNT

OTHER EXPENSES

DATE	DESCRIPTION	AMOUNT

TOTAL:

Weekly
BUDGET PLAN

WEEK: ______________________

MONDAY AMOUNT: | EXPENSES:

TUESDAY AMOUNT: | EXPENSES:

WEDNESDAY AMOUNT: | EXPENSES:

THRUSDAY AMOUNT: | EXPENSES:

FRIDAY AMOUNT: | EXPENSES:

SATURDAY AMOUNT: | EXPENSES:

SUNDAY AMOUNT:1 | EXPENSES:

TOTAL:

Weekly
BUDGET PLAN

WEEK:

____

MONDAY AMOUNT: | EXPENSES:

TUESDAY
AMOUNT: | EXPENSES:

WEDNESDAY
AMOUNT: | EXPENSES:

THRUSDAY
AMOUNT: | EXPENSES:

FRIDAY AMOUNT: | EXPENSES:

SATURDAY
AMOUNT: | EXPENSES:

SUNDAY
AMOUNT:1 | EXPENSES:

TOTAL:

Weekly
BUDGET PLAN

WEEK: ___________________

MONDAY AMOUNT: | EXPENSES:

TUESDAY
AMOUNT: | EXPENSES:

WEDNESDAY
AMOUNT: | EXPENSES:

THRUSDAY
AMOUNT: | EXPENSES:

FRIDAY AMOUNT: | EXPENSES:

SATURDAY
AMOUNT: | EXPENSES:

SUNDAY
AMOUNT:1 | EXPENSES:

TOTAL:

Weekly
BUDGET PLAN

WEEK: _______________________

MONDAY AMOUNT: | EXPENSES:

TUESDAY AMOUNT: | EXPENSES:

WEDNESDAY AMOUNT: | EXPENSES:

THRUSDAY AMOUNT: | EXPENSES:

FRIDAY AMOUNT: | EXPENSES:

SATURDAY AMOUNT: | EXPENSES:

SUNDAY AMOUNT:1 | EXPENSES:

TOTAL:

FOR SPECIAL

notes

FOR SPECIAL

notes

2024 December

Sun	Mon	Tue	Wed	Thu	Fri	Sat
1	2	3	4	5	6	7
8	9	10	11	12	13	14
15	16	17	18	19	20	21
22	23	24	25	26	27	28
29	30	31				

Monthly
BUDGET PLAN

MONTH:

INCOME

DATE	DESCRIPTION	AMOUNT

FIXED EXPENSES

DATE	DESCRIPTION	AMOUNT

OTHER EXPENSES

DATE	DESCRIPTION	AMOUNT

TOTAL:

Weekly
BUDGET PLAN

WEEK: _______________

MONDAY AMOUNT: | EXPENSES:

TUESDAY AMOUNT: | EXPENSES:

WEDNESDAY AMOUNT: | EXPENSES:

THRUSDAY AMOUNT: | EXPENSES:

FRIDAY AMOUNT: | EXPENSES:

SATURDAY AMOUNT: | EXPENSES:

SUNDAY AMOUNT:1 | EXPENSES:

TOTAL:

Weekly
BUDGET PLAN

WEEK:

____

MONDAY AMOUNT: | EXPENSES:

TUESDAY AMOUNT: | EXPENSES:

WEDNESDAY AMOUNT: | EXPENSES:

THRUSDAY AMOUNT: | EXPENSES:

FRIDAY AMOUNT: | EXPENSES:

SATURDAY AMOUNT: | EXPENSES:

SUNDAY AMOUNT:1 | EXPENSES:

TOTAL:

Weekly
BUDGET PLAN

WEEK: ______________________

MONDAY AMOUNT: | EXPENSES:

TUESDAY
AMOUNT: | EXPENSES:

WEDNESDAY
AMOUNT: | EXPENSES:

THRUSDAY
AMOUNT: | EXPENSES:

FRIDAY AMOUNT: | EXPENSES:

SATURDAY
AMOUNT: | EXPENSES:

SUNDAY
AMOUNT:1 | EXPENSES:

TOTAL:

Weekly
BUDGET PLAN

WEEK:

____

MONDAY AMOUNT: | EXPENSES:

TUESDAY AMOUNT: | EXPENSES:

WEDNESDAY AMOUNT: | EXPENSES:

THRUSDAY AMOUNT: | EXPENSES:

FRIDAY AMOUNT: | EXPENSES:

SATURDAY AMOUNT: | EXPENSES:

SUNDAY AMOUNT:1 | EXPENSES:

TOTAL:

FOR SPECIAL

notes

FOR SPECIAL

notes

2025

January

MO	TU	WE	TH	FR	SA	SU
		1	2	3	4	5
6	7	8	9	10	11	12
13	14	15	16	17	18	19
20	21	22	23	24	25	26
27	28	29	30	31		

February

MO	TU	WE	TH	FR	SA	SU
					1	2
3	4	5	6	7	8	9
10	11	12	13	14	15	16
17	18	19	20	21	22	23
24	25	26	27	28		

March

MO	TU	WE	TH	FR	SA	SU
					1	2
3	4	5	6	7	8	9
10	11	12	13	14	15	16
17	18	19	20	21	22	23
24	25	26	27	28	29	30
31						

April

MO	TU	WE	TH	FR	SA	SU
	1	2	3	4	5	6
7	8	9	10	11	12	13
14	15	16	17	18	19	20
21	22	23	24	25	26	27
28	29	30				

May

MO	TU	WE	TH	FR	SA	SU
			1	2	3	4
5	6	7	8	9	10	11
12	13	14	15	16	17	18
19	20	21	22	23	24	25
26	27	28	29	30	31	

June

MO	TU	WE	TH	FR	SA	SU
						1
2	3	4	5	6	7	8
9	10	11	12	13	14	15
16	17	18	19	20	21	22
23	24	25	26	27	28	29
30						

July

MO	TU	WE	TH	FR	SA	SU
	1	2	3	4	5	6
7	8	9	10	11	12	13
14	15	16	17	18	19	20
21	22	23	24	25	26	27
28	29	30	31			

August

MO	TU	WE	TH	FR	SA	SU
				1	2	3
4	5	6	7	8	9	10
11	12	13	14	15	16	17
18	19	20	21	22	23	24
25	26	27	28	29	30	31

September

MO	TU	WE	TH	FR	SA	SU
1	2	3	4	5	6	7
8	9	10	11	12	13	14
15	16	17	18	19	20	21
22	23	24	25	26	27	28
29	30					

October

MO	TU	WE	TH	FR	SA	SU
	1	2	3	4	5	
6	7	8	9	10	11	12
13	14	15	16	17	18	19
20	21	22	23	24	25	26
27	28	29	30	31		

November

MO	TU	WE	TH	FR	SA	SU
					1	2
3	4	5	6	7	8	9
10	11	12	13	14	15	16
17	18	19	20	21	22	23
24	25	26	27	28	29	30

December

MO	TU	WE	TH	FR	SA	SU
1	2	3	4	5	6	7
8	9	10	11	12	13	14
15	16	17	18	19	20	21
22	23	24	25	26	27	28
29	30	31				

Some things have to end for better things to begin

2025 January

Sun	Mon	Tue	Wed	Thu	Fri	Sat
			1	2	3	4
5	6	7	8	9	10	11
12	13	14	15	16	17	18
19	20	21	22	23	24	25
26	27	28	29	30	31	

Monthly
BUDGET PLAN

MONTH:

____

INCOME

DATE	DESCRIPTION	AMOUNT

FIXED EXPENSES

DATE	DESCRIPTION	AMOUNT

OTHER EXPENSES

DATE	DESCRIPTION	AMOUNT

TOTAL:

WEEK:

____

| MONDAY AMOUNT: | | EXPENSES: |

| TUESDAY AMOUNT: | | EXPENSES: |

| WEDNESDAY AMOUNT: | | EXPENSES: |

| THRUSDAY AMOUNT: | | EXPENSES: |

| FRIDAY AMOUNT: | | EXPENSES: |

| SATURDAY AMOUNT: | | EXPENSES: |

| SUNDAY AMOUNT:1 | | EXPENSES: |

TOTAL:

Weekly
BUDGET PLAN

WEEK:

____

MONDAY AMOUNT: | EXPENSES:

TUESDAY AMOUNT: | EXPENSES:

WEDNESDAY AMOUNT: | EXPENSES:

THRUSDAY AMOUNT: | EXPENSES:

FRIDAY AMOUNT: | EXPENSES:

SATURDAY AMOUNT: | EXPENSES:

SUNDAY AMOUNT:1 | EXPENSES:

TOTAL:

WEEK:

____

MONDAY AMOUNT: EXPENSES:

TUESDAY AMOUNT: EXPENSES:

WEDNESDAY AMOUNT: EXPENSES:

THRUSDAY AMOUNT: EXPENSES:

FRIDAY AMOUNT: EXPENSES:

SATURDAY AMOUNT: EXPENSES:

SUNDAY AMOUNT:1   EXPENSES:

TOTAL:

FOR SPECIAL
notes

notes

WEEK:

MONDAY AMOUNT:	EXPENSES:

TUESDAY AMOUNT:	EXPENSES:

WEDNESDAY AMOUNT:	EXPENSES:

THRUSDAY AMOUNT:	EXPENSES:

FRIDAY AMOUNT:	EXPENSES:

SATURDAY AMOUNT:	EXPENSES:

SUNDAY AMOUNT:1	EXPENSES:

TOTAL:

2025 February

Sun	Mon	Tue	Wed	Thu	Fri	Sat
						1
2	3	4	5	6	7	8
9	10	11	12	13	14	15
16	17	18	19	20	21	22
23	24	25	26	27	28	

Monthly
BUDGET PLAN

MONTH: _______________________

INCOME

DATE	DESCRIPTION	AMOUNT

FIXED EXPENSES

DATE	DESCRIPTION	AMOUNT

OTHER EXPENSES

DATE	DESCRIPTION	AMOUNT

TOTAL:

Weekly
BUDGET PLAN

WEEK:

MONDAY AMOUNT: | EXPENSES:

TUESDAY AMOUNT: | EXPENSES:

WEDNESDAY AMOUNT: | EXPENSES:

THRUSDAY AMOUNT: | EXPENSES:

FRIDAY AMOUNT: | EXPENSES:

SATURDAY AMOUNT: | EXPENSES:

SUNDAY AMOUNT:1 | EXPENSES:

TOTAL:

WEEK:

MONDAY AMOUNT: EXPENSES:

TUESDAY AMOUNT: EXPENSES:

WEDNESDAY AMOUNT: EXPENSES:

THRUSDAY AMOUNT: EXPENSES:

FRIDAY AMOUNT: EXPENSES:

SATURDAY AMOUNT: EXPENSES:

SUNDAY AMOUNT:1   EXPENSES:

TOTAL:

WEEK:

____

| MONDAY AMOUNT: | | EXPENSES: |

| TUESDAY AMOUNT: | | EXPENSES: |

| WEDNESDAY AMOUNT: | | EXPENSES: |

| THRUSDAY AMOUNT: | | EXPENSES: |

| FRIDAY AMOUNT: | | EXPENSES: |

| SATURDAY AMOUNT: | | EXPENSES: |

| SUNDAY AMOUNT:1 | | EXPENSES: |

TOTAL:

Weekly
BUDGET PLAN

WEEK:

MONDAY AMOUNT: | EXPENSES:

TUESDAY AMOUNT: | EXPENSES:

WEDNESDAY AMOUNT: | EXPENSES:

THRUSDAY AMOUNT: | EXPENSES:

FRIDAY AMOUNT: | EXPENSES:

SATURDAY AMOUNT: | EXPENSES:

SUNDAY AMOUNT:1 | EXPENSES:

TOTAL:

FOR SPECIAL
notes

2025 March

Sun	Mon	Tue	Wed	Thu	Fri	Sat
						1
2	3	4	5	6	7	8
9	10	11	12	13	14	15
16	17	18	19	20	21	22
23	24	25	26	27	28	29
30	31					

Monthly
BUDGET PLAN

MONTH: ___________________

INCOME

DATE	DESCRIPTION	AMOUNT

FIXED EXPENSES

DATE	DESCRIPTION	AMOUNT

OTHER EXPENSES

DATE	DESCRIPTION	AMOUNT

TOTAL:

WEEK:

MONDAY AMOUNT: | EXPENSES:

TUESDAY AMOUNT: | EXPENSES:

WEDNESDAY AMOUNT: | EXPENSES:

THRUSDAY AMOUNT: | EXPENSES:

FRIDAY AMOUNT: | EXPENSES:

SATURDAY AMOUNT: | EXPENSES:

SUNDAY AMOUNT:1 | EXPENSES:

TOTAL:

 Weekly
BUDGET PLAN

WEEK:

____

MONDAY AMOUNT:	EXPENSES:

TUESDAY AMOUNT:	EXPENSES:

WEDNESDAY AMOUNT:	EXPENSES:

THRUSDAY AMOUNT:	EXPENSES:

FRIDAY AMOUNT:	EXPENSES:

SATURDAY AMOUNT:	EXPENSES:

SUNDAY AMOUNT:1	EXPENSES:

TOTAL:

Weekly
BUDGET PLAN

WEEK:

____

MONDAY AMOUNT: EXPENSES:

TUESDAY AMOUNT: EXPENSES:

WEDNESDAY AMOUNT: EXPENSES:

THRUSDAY AMOUNT: EXPENSES:

FRIDAY AMOUNT: EXPENSES:

SATURDAY AMOUNT: EXPENSES:

SUNDAY AMOUNT:1   EXPENSES:

TOTAL:

WEEK: _______________________

MONDAY AMOUNT: | EXPENSES:

TUESDAY AMOUNT: | EXPENSES:

WEDNESDAY AMOUNT: | EXPENSES:

THRUSDAY AMOUNT: | EXPENSES:

FRIDAY AMOUNT: | EXPENSES:

SATURDAY AMOUNT: | EXPENSES:

SUNDAY AMOUNT:1 | EXPENSES:

TOTAL:

FOR SPECIAL

notes

FOR SPECIAL
notes

2025 April

Sun	Mon	Tue	Wed	Thu	Fri	Sat
		1	2	3	4	5
6	7	8	9	10	11	12
13	14	15	16	17	18	19
20	21	22	23	24	25	26
27	28	29	30			

Monthly
BUDGET PLAN

MONTH:

____

INCOME

DATE	DESCRIPTION	AMOUNT

FIXED EXPENSES

DATE	DESCRIPTION	AMOUNT

OTHER EXPENSES

DATE	DESCRIPTION	AMOUNT

TOTAL:

Weekly
BUDGET PLAN

WEEK:

MONDAY AMOUNT: | EXPENSES:

TUESDAY AMOUNT: | EXPENSES:

WEDNESDAY AMOUNT: | EXPENSES:

THRUSDAY AMOUNT: | EXPENSES:

FRIDAY AMOUNT: | EXPENSES:

SATURDAY AMOUNT: | EXPENSES:

SUNDAY AMOUNT:1 | EXPENSES:

TOTAL:

WEEK:

MONDAY AMOUNT:	EXPENSES:

TUESDAY AMOUNT:	EXPENSES:

WEDNESDAY AMOUNT:	EXPENSES:

THRUSDAY AMOUNT:	EXPENSES:

FRIDAY AMOUNT:	EXPENSES:

SATURDAY AMOUNT:	EXPENSES:

SUNDAY AMOUNT:1	EXPENSES:

TOTAL:

WEEK:

MONDAY AMOUNT: | EXPENSES:

TUESDAY AMOUNT: | EXPENSES:

WEDNESDAY AMOUNT: | EXPENSES:

THRUSDAY AMOUNT: | EXPENSES:

FRIDAY AMOUNT: | EXPENSES:

SATURDAY AMOUNT: | EXPENSES:

SUNDAY AMOUNT:1 | EXPENSES:

TOTAL:

WEEK:

MONDAY AMOUNT: EXPENSES:

TUESDAY AMOUNT: EXPENSES:

WEDNESDAY AMOUNT: EXPENSES:

THRUSDAY AMOUNT: EXPENSES:

FRIDAY AMOUNT: EXPENSES:

SATURDAY AMOUNT: EXPENSES:

SUNDAY AMOUNT:1   EXPENSES:

TOTAL:

FOR SPECIAL

notes

2025
May

Sun	Mon	Tue	Wed	Thu	Fri	Sat
				1	2	3
4	5	6	7	8	9	10
11	12	13	14	15	16	17
18	19	20	21	22	23	24
25	26	27	28	29	30	31

Monthly
BUDGET PLAN

MONTH: _______________________

INCOME

DATE	DESCRIPTION	AMOUNT

FIXED EXPENSES

DATE	DESCRIPTION	AMOUNT

OTHER EXPENSES

DATE	DESCRIPTION	AMOUNT

TOTAL:

WEEK:

MONDAY AMOUNT: EXPENSES:

TUESDAY AMOUNT: EXPENSES:

WEDNESDAY AMOUNT: EXPENSES:

THRUSDAY AMOUNT: EXPENSES:

FRIDAY AMOUNT: EXPENSES:

SATURDAY AMOUNT: EXPENSES:

SUNDAY AMOUNT:1   EXPENSES:

TOTAL:

WEEK:

MONDAY AMOUNT: | EXPENSES:

TUESDAY AMOUNT: | EXPENSES:

WEDNESDAY AMOUNT: | EXPENSES:

THRUSDAY AMOUNT: | EXPENSES:

FRIDAY AMOUNT: | EXPENSES:

SATURDAY AMOUNT: | EXPENSES:

SUNDAY AMOUNT:1 | EXPENSES:

TOTAL:

WEEK:

MONDAY AMOUNT: EXPENSES:

TUESDAY AMOUNT: EXPENSES:

WEDNESDAY AMOUNT: EXPENSES:

THRUSDAY AMOUNT: EXPENSES:

FRIDAY AMOUNT: EXPENSES:

SATURDAY AMOUNT: EXPENSES:

SUNDAY AMOUNT:1   EXPENSES:

TOTAL:

WEEK:

MONDAY AMOUNT: | EXPENSES:

TUESDAY AMOUNT: | EXPENSES:

WEDNESDAY AMOUNT: | EXPENSES:

THRUSDAY AMOUNT: | EXPENSES:

FRIDAY AMOUNT: | EXPENSES:

SATURDAY AMOUNT: | EXPENSES:

SUNDAY AMOUNT:1 | EXPENSES:

TOTAL:

FOR SPECIAL

notes

FOR SPECIAL
notes

2025
June

Sun	Mon	Tue	Wed	Thu	Fri	Sat
1	2	3	4	5	6	7
8	9	10	11	12	13	14
15	16	17	18	19	20	21
22	23	24	25	26	27	28
29	30					

Monthly
BUDGET PLAN

MONTH:

INCOME

DATE	DESCRIPTION	AMOUNT

FIXED EXPENSES

DATE	DESCRIPTION	AMOUNT

OTHER EXPENSES

DATE	DESCRIPTION	AMOUNT

TOTAL:

WEEK:

MONDAY AMOUNT:

EXPENSES:

TUESDAY AMOUNT:

EXPENSES:

WEDNESDAY AMOUNT:

EXPENSES:

THRUSDAY AMOUNT:

EXPENSES:

FRIDAY AMOUNT:

EXPENSES:

SATURDAY AMOUNT:

EXPENSES:

SUNDAY AMOUNT:1

EXPENSES:

TOTAL:

Weekly
BUDGET PLAN

WEEK:

| MONDAY AMOUNT: | EXPENSES: |

| TUESDAY AMOUNT: | EXPENSES: |

| WEDNESDAY AMOUNT: | EXPENSES: |

| THRUSDAY AMOUNT: | EXPENSES: |

| FRIDAY AMOUNT: | EXPENSES: |

| SATURDAY AMOUNT: | EXPENSES: |

| SUNDAY AMOUNT:1 | EXPENSES: |

TOTAL:

WEEK:

____

MONDAY AMOUNT:		EXPENSES:

TUESDAY AMOUNT:		EXPENSES:

WEDNESDAY AMOUNT:		EXPENSES:

THRUSDAY AMOUNT:		EXPENSES:

FRIDAY AMOUNT:		EXPENSES:

SATURDAY AMOUNT:		EXPENSES:

SUNDAY AMOUNT:1		EXPENSES:

TOTAL:

Weekly
BUDGET PLAN

WEEK:

MONDAY AMOUNT: | EXPENSES:

TUESDAY AMOUNT: | EXPENSES:

WEDNESDAY AMOUNT: | EXPENSES:

THRUSDAY AMOUNT: | EXPENSES:

FRIDAY AMOUNT: | EXPENSES:

SATURDAY AMOUNT: | EXPENSES:

SUNDAY AMOUNT:1 | EXPENSES:

TOTAL:

2025
July

Sun	Mon	Tue	Wed	Thu	Fri	Sat
		1	2	3	4	5
6	7	8	9	10	11	12
13	14	15	16	17	18	19
20	21	22	23	24	25	26
27	28	29	30	31		

Monthly
BUDGET PLAN

MONTH:

____

INCOME

DATE	DESCRIPTION	AMOUNT

FIXED EXPENSES

DATE	DESCRIPTION	AMOUNT

OTHER EXPENSES

DATE	DESCRIPTION	AMOUNT

TOTAL:

WEEK:

MONDAY AMOUNT: | EXPENSES:

TUESDAY AMOUNT: | EXPENSES:

WEDNESDAY AMOUNT: | EXPENSES:

THRUSDAY AMOUNT: | EXPENSES:

FRIDAY AMOUNT: | EXPENSES:

SATURDAY AMOUNT: | EXPENSES:

SUNDAY AMOUNT:1 | EXPENSES:

TOTAL:

WEEK:

MONDAY AMOUNT: | EXPENSES:

TUESDAY AMOUNT: | EXPENSES:

WEDNESDAY AMOUNT: | EXPENSES:

THRUSDAY AMOUNT: | EXPENSES:

FRIDAY AMOUNT: | EXPENSES:

SATURDAY AMOUNT: | EXPENSES:

SUNDAY AMOUNT:1 | EXPENSES:

TOTAL:

Weekly
BUDGET PLAN

WEEK:

MONDAY AMOUNT: EXPENSES:

TUESDAY AMOUNT: EXPENSES:

WEDNESDAY AMOUNT: EXPENSES:

THRUSDAY AMOUNT: EXPENSES:

FRIDAY AMOUNT: EXPENSES:

SATURDAY AMOUNT: EXPENSES:

SUNDAY AMOUNT:1   EXPENSES:

TOTAL:

WEEK:

MONDAY AMOUNT: EXPENSES:

TUESDAY AMOUNT: EXPENSES:

WEDNESDAY AMOUNT: EXPENSES:

THRUSDAY AMOUNT: EXPENSES:

FRIDAY AMOUNT: EXPENSES:

SATURDAY AMOUNT: EXPENSES:

SUNDAY AMOUNT:1   EXPENSES:

TOTAL:

notes

FOR SPECIAL

2025
August

Sun	Mon	Tue	Wed	Thu	Fri	Sat
					1	2
3	4	5	6	7	8	9
10	11	12	13	14	15	16
17	18	19	20	21	22	23
24	25	26	27	28	29	30
31						

Monthly
BUDGET PLAN

MONTH: ___________________

INCOME

DATE	DESCRIPTION	AMOUNT

FIXED EXPENSES

DATE	DESCRIPTION	AMOUNT

OTHER EXPENSES

DATE	DESCRIPTION	AMOUNT

TOTAL:

Weekly
BUDGET PLAN

WEEK:

MONDAY AMOUNT:

EXPENSES:

TUESDAY AMOUNT:

EXPENSES:

WEDNESDAY AMOUNT:

EXPENSES:

THRUSDAY AMOUNT:

EXPENSES:

FRIDAY AMOUNT:

EXPENSES:

SATURDAY AMOUNT:

EXPENSES:

SUNDAY AMOUNT:1

EXPENSES:

TOTAL:

WEEK:

MONDAY AMOUNT: | EXPENSES:

TUESDAY AMOUNT: | EXPENSES:

WEDNESDAY AMOUNT: | EXPENSES:

THRUSDAY AMOUNT: | EXPENSES:

FRIDAY AMOUNT: | EXPENSES:

SATURDAY AMOUNT: | EXPENSES:

SUNDAY AMOUNT:1 | EXPENSES:

TOTAL:

Weekly
BUDGET PLAN

WEEK:

____

MONDAY AMOUNT: | EXPENSES:

TUESDAY AMOUNT: | EXPENSES:

WEDNESDAY AMOUNT: | EXPENSES:

THRUSDAY AMOUNT: | EXPENSES:

FRIDAY AMOUNT: | EXPENSES:

SATURDAY AMOUNT: | EXPENSES:

SUNDAY AMOUNT:1 | EXPENSES:

TOTAL:

WEEK:

MONDAY AMOUNT: | EXPENSES:

TUESDAY AMOUNT: | EXPENSES:

WEDNESDAY AMOUNT: | EXPENSES:

THRUSDAY AMOUNT: | EXPENSES:

FRIDAY AMOUNT: | EXPENSES:

SATURDAY AMOUNT: | EXPENSES:

SUNDAY AMOUNT:1 | EXPENSES:

TOTAL:

notes

notes

2025 September

Sun	Mon	Tue	Wed	Thu	Fri	Sat
	1	2	3	4	5	6
7	8	9	10	11	12	13
14	15	16	17	18	19	20
21	22	23	24	25	26	27
28	29	30				

Monthly
BUDGET PLAN

MONTH:

____

INCOME

DATE	DESCRIPTION	AMOUNT

FIXED EXPENSES

DATE	DESCRIPTION	AMOUNT

OTHER EXPENSES

DATE	DESCRIPTION	AMOUNT

TOTAL:

Weekly
BUDGET PLAN

WEEK:

____

| MONDAY AMOUNT: | | EXPENSES: |

| TUESDAY AMOUNT: | | EXPENSES: |

| WEDNESDAY AMOUNT: | | EXPENSES: |

| THRUSDAY AMOUNT: | | EXPENSES: |

| FRIDAY AMOUNT: | | EXPENSES: |

| SATURDAY AMOUNT: | | EXPENSES: |

| SUNDAY AMOUNT:1 | | EXPENSES: |

TOTAL:

Weekly
BUDGET PLAN

WEEK:

MONDAY AMOUNT: EXPENSES:

TUESDAY AMOUNT: EXPENSES:

WEDNESDAY AMOUNT: EXPENSES:

THRUSDAY AMOUNT: EXPENSES:

FRIDAY AMOUNT: EXPENSES:

SATURDAY AMOUNT: EXPENSES:

SUNDAY AMOUNT:1   EXPENSES:

TOTAL:

WEEK:

____

MONDAY AMOUNT: | EXPENSES:

TUESDAY AMOUNT: | EXPENSES:

WEDNESDAY AMOUNT: | EXPENSES:

THRUSDAY AMOUNT: | EXPENSES:

FRIDAY AMOUNT: | EXPENSES:

SATURDAY AMOUNT: | EXPENSES:

SUNDAY AMOUNT:1 | EXPENSES:

TOTAL:

WEEK:

____

MONDAY AMOUNT: | EXPENSES:

TUESDAY AMOUNT: | EXPENSES:

WEDNESDAY AMOUNT: | EXPENSES:

THRUSDAY AMOUNT: | EXPENSES:

FRIDAY AMOUNT: | EXPENSES:

SATURDAY AMOUNT: | EXPENSES:

SUNDAY AMOUNT:1 | EXPENSES:

TOTAL:

notes

FOR SPECIAL *notes*

2025 October

Sun	Mon	Tue	Wed	Thu	Fri	Sat
			1	2	3	4
5	6	7	8	9	10	11
12	13	14	15	16	17	18
19	20	21	22	23	24	25
26	27	28	29	30	31	

Monthly
BUDGET PLAN

MONTH: ___________________________

INCOME

DATE	DESCRIPTION	AMOUNT

FIXED EXPENSES

DATE	DESCRIPTION	AMOUNT

OTHER EXPENSES

DATE	DESCRIPTION	AMOUNT

TOTAL:

Weekly
BUDGET PLAN

WEEK:

MONDAY AMOUNT:

EXPENSES:

TUESDAY AMOUNT:

EXPENSES:

WEDNESDAY AMOUNT:

EXPENSES:

THRUSDAY AMOUNT:

EXPENSES:

FRIDAY AMOUNT:

EXPENSES:

SATURDAY AMOUNT:

EXPENSES:

SUNDAY AMOUNT:1

EXPENSES:

TOTAL:

Weekly BUDGET PLAN

WEEK:

| MONDAY AMOUNT: | EXPENSES: |

| TUESDAY AMOUNT: | EXPENSES: |

| WEDNESDAY AMOUNT: | EXPENSES: |

| THRUSDAY AMOUNT: | EXPENSES: |

| FRIDAY AMOUNT: | EXPENSES: |

| SATURDAY AMOUNT: | EXPENSES: |

| SUNDAY AMOUNT:1 | EXPENSES: |

TOTAL:

WEEK:

MONDAY AMOUNT: | EXPENSES:

TUESDAY AMOUNT: | EXPENSES:

WEDNESDAY AMOUNT: | EXPENSES:

THRUSDAY AMOUNT: | EXPENSES:

FRIDAY AMOUNT: | EXPENSES:

SATURDAY AMOUNT: | EXPENSES:

SUNDAY AMOUNT:1 | EXPENSES:

TOTAL:

WEEK:

MONDAY AMOUNT:

EXPENSES:

TUESDAY AMOUNT:

EXPENSES:

WEDNESDAY AMOUNT:

EXPENSES:

THRUSDAY AMOUNT:

EXPENSES:

FRIDAY AMOUNT:

EXPENSES:

SATURDAY AMOUNT:

EXPENSES:

SUNDAY AMOUNT:1

EXPENSES:

TOTAL:

FOR SPECIAL *notes*

FOR SPECIAL

notes

2025 November

Sun	Mon	Tue	Wed	Thu	Fri	Sat
						1
2	3	4	5	6	7	8
9	10	11	12	13	14	15
16	17	18	19	20	21	22
23	24	25	26	27	28	29
30						

Monthly
BUDGET PLAN

MONTH:

INCOME

DATE	DESCRIPTION	AMOUNT

FIXED EXPENSES		
DATE	DESCRIPTION	AMOUNT

OTHER EXPENSES		
DATE	DESCRIPTION	AMOUNT

TOTAL:

Weekly
BUDGET PLAN

WEEK:

MONDAY AMOUNT:

EXPENSES:

TUESDAY AMOUNT:

EXPENSES:

WEDNESDAY AMOUNT:

EXPENSES:

THRUSDAY AMOUNT:

EXPENSES:

FRIDAY AMOUNT:

EXPENSES:

SATURDAY AMOUNT:

EXPENSES:

SUNDAY AMOUNT:1

EXPENSES:

TOTAL:

WEEK:

| MONDAY AMOUNT: | EXPENSES: |

| TUESDAY AMOUNT: | EXPENSES: |

| WEDNESDAY AMOUNT: | EXPENSES: |

| THRUSDAY AMOUNT: | EXPENSES: |

| FRIDAY AMOUNT: | EXPENSES: |

| SATURDAY AMOUNT: | EXPENSES: |

| SUNDAY AMOUNT:1 | EXPENSES: |

TOTAL:

WEEK: _______________

MONDAY AMOUNT: EXPENSES:

TUESDAY AMOUNT: EXPENSES:

WEDNESDAY AMOUNT: EXPENSES:

THRUSDAY AMOUNT: EXPENSES:

FRIDAY AMOUNT: EXPENSES:

SATURDAY AMOUNT: EXPENSES:

SUNDAY AMOUNT:1 EXPENSES:

TOTAL:

Weekly
BUDGET PLAN

WEEK:

MONDAY AMOUNT:

EXPENSES:

TUESDAY AMOUNT:

EXPENSES:

WEDNESDAY AMOUNT:

EXPENSES:

THRUSDAY AMOUNT:

EXPENSES:

FRIDAY AMOUNT:

EXPENSES:

SATURDAY AMOUNT:

EXPENSES:

SUNDAY AMOUNT:1

EXPENSES:

TOTAL:

FOR SPECIAL

notes

FOR SPECIAL

notes

2025 December

Sun	Mon	Tue	Wed	Thu	Fri	Sat
	1	2	3	4	5	6
7	8	9	10	11	12	13
14	15	16	17	18	19	20
21	22	23	24	25	26	27
28	29	30	31			

Monthly
BUDGET PLAN

MONTH:

____

INCOME

DATE	DESCRIPTION	AMOUNT

FIXED EXPENSES

DATE	DESCRIPTION	AMOUNT

OTHER EXPENSES

DATE	DESCRIPTION	AMOUNT

TOTAL:

WEEK:

____

MONDAY AMOUNT: EXPENSES:

TUESDAY AMOUNT: EXPENSES:

WEDNESDAY AMOUNT: EXPENSES:

THRUSDAY AMOUNT: EXPENSES:

FRIDAY AMOUNT: EXPENSES:

SATURDAY AMOUNT: EXPENSES:

SUNDAY AMOUNT:1   EXPENSES:

TOTAL:

Weekly
BUDGET PLAN

WEEK:

MONDAY AMOUNT: | EXPENSES:

TUESDAY AMOUNT: | EXPENSES:

WEDNESDAY AMOUNT: | EXPENSES:

THRUSDAY AMOUNT: | EXPENSES:

FRIDAY AMOUNT: | EXPENSES:

SATURDAY AMOUNT: | EXPENSES:

SUNDAY AMOUNT:1 | EXPENSES:

TOTAL:

Weekly
BUDGET PLAN

WEEK:

MONDAY AMOUNT: | EXPENSES:

TUESDAY AMOUNT: | EXPENSES:

WEDNESDAY AMOUNT: | EXPENSES:

THRUSDAY AMOUNT: | EXPENSES:

FRIDAY AMOUNT: | EXPENSES:

SATURDAY AMOUNT: | EXPENSES:

SUNDAY AMOUNT:1 | EXPENSES:

TOTAL:

WEEK:

MONDAY AMOUNT: | EXPENSES:

TUESDAY AMOUNT: | EXPENSES:

WEDNESDAY AMOUNT: | EXPENSES:

THRUSDAY AMOUNT: | EXPENSES:

FRIDAY AMOUNT: | EXPENSES:

SATURDAY AMOUNT: | EXPENSES:

SUNDAY AMOUNT:1 | EXPENSES:

TOTAL:

FOR SPECIAL
notes

DEBT SNOWBALL TRACKER

Date	Starting Balance	Debt 1	Debt 2	Debt 3

Notes

DEBT SNOWBALL TRACKER

Date	Starting Balance	Debt 1	Debt 2	Debt 3

Notes

DEBT SNOWBALL TRACKER

Date	Starting Balance	Debt 1	Debt 2	Debt 3

Notes

DEBT SNOWBALL TRACKER

Date	Starting Balance	Debt 1	Debt 2	Debt 3

Notes

DEBT SNOWBALL TRACKER

Date	Starting Balance	Debt 1	Debt 2	Debt 3

Notes

DEBT SNOWBALL TRACKER

Date	Starting Balance	Debt 1	Debt 2	Debt 3

Notes

DEBT SNOWBALL TRACKER

Date	Starting Balance	Debt 1	Debt 2	Debt 3

Notes